CELLO

T0088368

for STRINGS

by HARVEY S. WHISTLER and HERMAN A. HUMMEL

CONTENTS

RUBANK®

HAL•LEONARD®
CORPORATION
7777 W BLUEMOUND Rd. P.O. Box 13819 MILWAUKEE, WI 53213

Units		PAGE NUMBERS		
		Strings	Piano	Score
1-16	Key of C Major	2	2	4
17-32	Key of G Major	4	5	10
33-48	Key of D Major	6	8	16
49-64	Key of A Major	8	11	22
65-80	Key of F Major	10	14	28
81-96	Key of B♭ Major	12	17	34
97-112	Key of E♭ Major	14	20	40
113-120	Chromatic Scales	16	23	46

Key of C Major

Détaché Scale

Use détaché bowing in (1) LOWER HALF, (2) MIDDLE, and (3) UPPER HALF of bow.

Relative Minor Scales and Chords

Use détaché bowing in (1) LOWER HALF, (2) MIDDLE, and (3) UPPER HALF of bow.

Scales and Chords in Eighth Notes

Also practice (1) slurring each two notes, and (2) slurring each four notes.

Staccato Scales

Use short strokes in (1) LOWER HALF, and (2) MIDDLE of bow.

Scale and Chord in 6/8 Meter

Triplets

Use (1) LOWER HALF, (2) MIDDLE, and (3) UPPER HALF of bow.

Dotted Eighth and Sixteenth Notes

Use (1) LOWER HALF, (2) MIDDLE, and (3) UPPER HALF of bow.

Be sure to start UP BOW. Play at extreme tip of stick, using about four inches of hair.

AT POINT

Articulated Scales and Chords

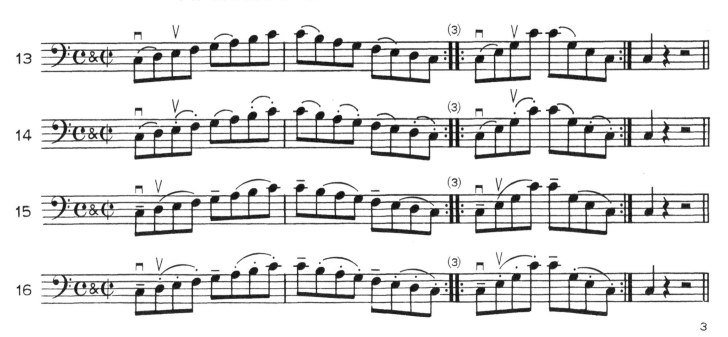

Key of G Major
Détaché Scale

17 Scale of G   (5) Chord of G

Use détaché bowing in (1) LOWER HALF, (2) MIDDLE, and (3) UPPER HALF of bow.

Relative Minor Scales and Chords

Use détaché bowing in (1) LOWER HALF, (2) MIDDLE, and (3) UPPER HALF of bow.

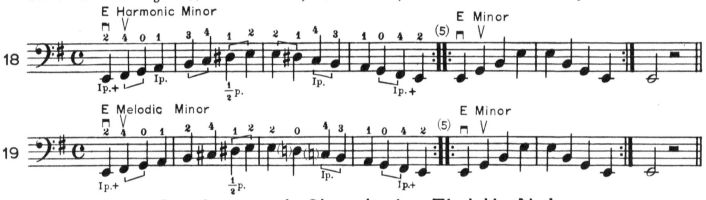

Scales and Chords in Eighth Notes

Also practice (1) slurring each two notes, and (2) slurring each four notes.

Staccato Scales

Use short strokes in (1) LOWER HALF, and (2) MIDDLE of bow.

Scale and Chord in 6/8 Meter

Triplets

Use (1) LOWER HALF, (2) MIDDLE, and (3) UPPER HALF of bow.

Dotted Eighth and Sixteenth Notes

Use (1) LOWER HALF, (2) MIDDLE, and (3) UPPER HALF of bow.

Be sure to start UP BOW. Play at extreme tip of stick, using about four inches of hair.

Articulated Scales and Chords

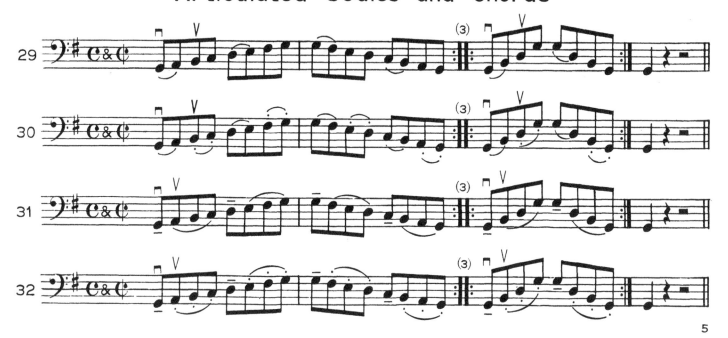

Key of D Major

Détaché Scale

Use détaché bowing in (1) LOWER HALF, (2) MIDDLE, and (3) UPPER HALF of bow.

Relative Minor Scales and Chords

Use détaché bowing in (1) LOWER HALF, (2) MIDDLE, and (3) UPPER HALF of bow.

Scales and Chords in Eighth Notes

Also practice (1) slurring each two notes, and (2) slurring each four notes.

Staccato Scales

Use short strokes in (1) LOWER HALF, and (2) MIDDLE of bow.

Scale and Chord in 6/8 Meter

Triplets

Use (1) LOWER HALF, (2) MIDDLE, and (3) UPPER HALF of bow.

Dotted Eighth and Sixteenth Notes

Use (1) LOWER HALF, (2) MIDDLE, and (3) UPPER HALF of bow.

Be sure to start UP BOW. Play at extreme tip of stick, using about four inches of hair.

AT POINT

Articulated Scales and Chords

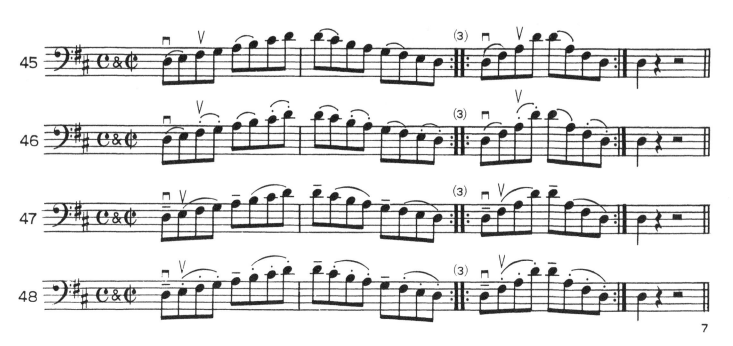

Key of A Major

Détaché Scale

49 Scale of A Chord of A (5)

Use détaché bowing in (1) LOWER HALF, (2) MIDDLE, and (3) UPPER HALF of bow.

Relative Minor Scales and Chords

Use détaché bowing in (1) LOWER HALF, (2) MIDDLE, and (3) UPPER HALF of bow.

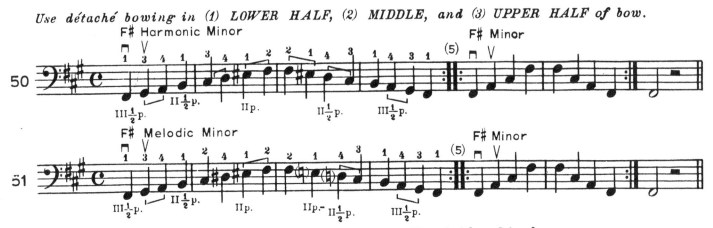

50 F# Harmonic Minor F# Minor (5)

51 F# Melodic Minor F# Minor (5)

Scales and Chords in Eighth Notes

Also practice (1) slurring each two notes, and (2) slurring each four notes.

52 A Major A Major (5)

53 F# Harmonic Minor F# Minor (5)

54 F# Melodic Minor F# Minor (5)

Staccato Scales

Use short strokes in (1) LOWER HALF, and (2) MIDDLE of bow.

55 simile (3)

56 (3)

Scale and Chord in 6/8 Meter

Triplets

Use (1) LOWER HALF, (2) MIDDLE, and (3) UPPER HALF of bow.

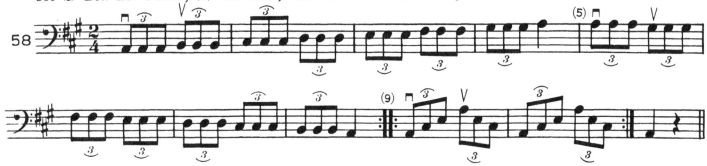

Dotted Eighth and Sixteenth Notes

Use (1) LOWER HALF, (2) MIDDLE, and (3) UPPER HALF of bow.

Be sure to start UP BOW. Play at extreme tip of stick, using about four inches of hair.

AT POINT

Articulated Scales and Chords

9

Key of F Major
Détaché Scale

65 Scale of F ... Chord of F ... (5)

Use détaché bowing in (1) LOWER HALF, (2) MIDDLE, and (3) UPPER HALF of bow.

Relative Minor Scales and Chords

Use détaché bowing in (1) LOWER HALF, (2) MIDDLE, and (3) UPPER HALF of bow.

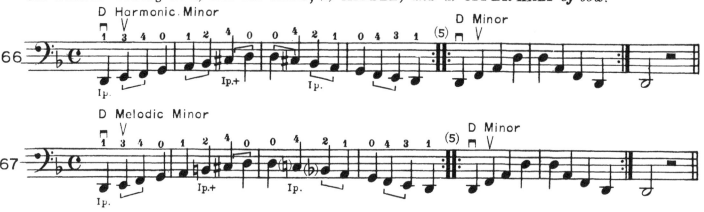

66 D Harmonic Minor ... D Minor ... (5)

67 D Melodic Minor ... D Minor ... (5)

Scales and Chords in Eighth Notes

Also practice (1) slurring each two notes, and (2) slurring each four notes.

68 F Major ... F Major ... (5)

69 D Harmonic Minor ... D Minor ... (5)

70 D Melodic Minor ... D Minor ... (5)

Staccato Scales

Use short strokes in (1) LOWER HALF, and (2) MIDDLE of bow.

71 simile ... (3)

72 (3)

Scale and Chord in 6/8 Meter

Triplets

Use (1) LOWER HALF, (2) MIDDLE, and (3) UPPER HALF of bow.

Dotted Eighth and Sixteenth Notes

Use (1) LOWER HALF, (2) MIDDLE, and (3) UPPER HALF of bow.

Be sure to start UP BOW. Play at extreme tip of stick, using about four inches of hair.

Articulated Scales and Chords

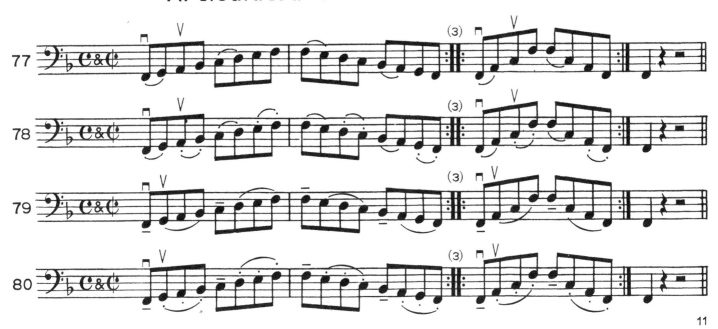

11

Key of B♭ Major

Détaché Scale

Use détaché bowing in (1) LOWER HALF, (2) MIDDLE, and (3) UPPER HALF of oow.

Relative Minor Scales and Chords

Use détaché bowing in (1) LOWER HALF, (2) MIDDLE, and (3) UPPER HALF of bow.

Scales and Chords in Eighth Notes

Also practice (1) slurring each two notes, and (2) slurring each four notes.

Staccato Scales

Use short strokes in (1) LOWER HALF, and (2) MIDDLE of bow.

Scale and Chord in 6/8 Meter

Triplets

Use (1) LOWER HALF, (2) MIDDLE, and (3) UPPER HALF of bow.

Dotted Eighth and Sixteenth Notes

Use (1) LOWER HALF, (2) MIDDLE, and (3) UPPER HALF of bow.

Be sure to start UP BOW. Play at extreme tip of stick, using about four inches of hair.

AT POINT

Articulated Scales and Chords

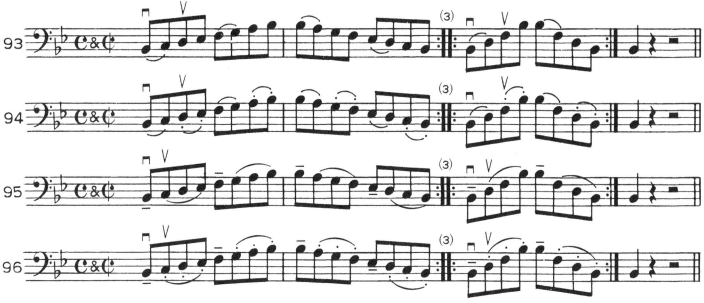

Key of E♭ Major

Détaché Scale

97

Use détaché bowing in (1) LOWER HALF, (2) MIDDLE, and (3) UPPER HALF of bow.

Relative Minor Scales and Chords

Use détaché bowing in (1) LOWER HALF, (2) MIDDLE, and (3) UPPER HALF of bow.

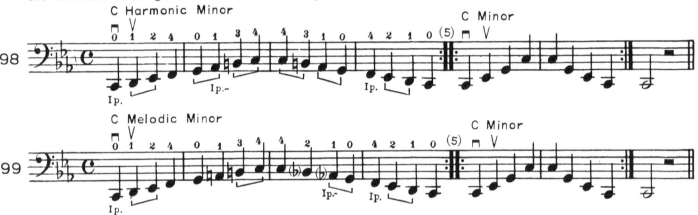

98

99

Scales and Chords in Eighth Notes

Also practice (1) slurring each two notes, and (2) slurring each four notes.

100

101

102

Staccato Scales

Use short strokes in (1) LOWER HALF, and (2) MIDDLE of bow.

103

104

Scale and Chord in 6/8 Meter

Triplets

Use (1) LOWER HALF, (2) MIDDLE, and (3) UPPER HALF of bow.

Dotted Eighth and Sixteenth Notes

Use (1) LOWER HALF, (2) MIDDLE, and (3) UPPER HALF of bow.

Be sure to start UP BOW. Play at extreme tip of stick, using about four inches of hair.

AT POINT

Articulated Scales and Chords

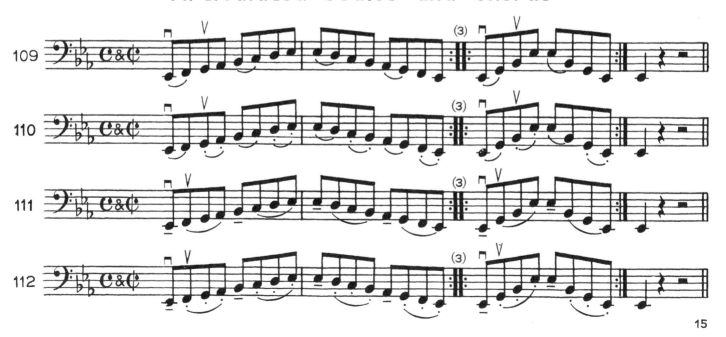

Chromatic Scales

FIRST POSITION FINGERING
(Above Notes)
Ascending from open string: 0-1-1-2-3-4-4
Descending from fourth finger: 4-4-3-2-1-1-0

Preferred fingerings are in POSITIONS and indicated below notes.

Extended Chromatic Scale

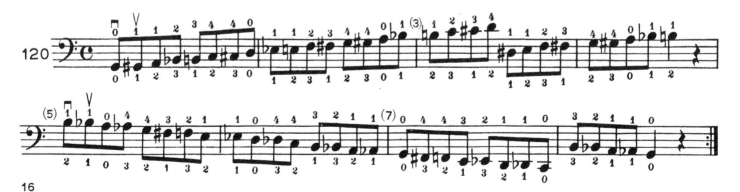